"It's only hubris if I fail" [1]
-- Julius Caesar (Roman General, Statesman, 100-44 B.C.)

Hubris is "a human vice"[2] relentlessly subjecting individuals to a continuous battle between humility and the intoxication of power. The greater danger of hubris, proposed to be an inherent natural human trait, rests in the negative aspects resulting from an individual unable to balance humility with power and embracing a leadership vision overshadowed by self-aggrandizement.[3] Hubris goes beyond the basic definition of arrogance, "an unwarrantable claim in respect of one's own importance,"[4] and dangerously merges with a belief in personal grandeur. This blended tragic flaw manifests as elevation of one's self while producing feelings of contempt for others. Built upon these two key elements, hubris leads to many perceptions internalized by the afflicted: a conflated self-ego, exalted speech built upon a royal 'we', actions chosen with a disproportionate concern for enhancing personal image, contempt for others, and isolation from opposition except from a higher being.[5]

History provides countless examples of arrogant individuals exhibiting impetuous, incompetent, impulsive, inattentive, and reckless behaviors. However, the impact of hubris in history, where significant opportunities are squandered leading to ruin and collapse, couples arrogance in leaders with a fierce streak of narcissism without mediation or opposition. In order for the consequence of hubris to occur, a leader must possess the underlying character flaw of hubris, so that the decisions and behavior are altered accordingly when power is gained.

Military failures resulting from the fatal flaw of hubris have profound costs and combatant commanders must conduct an initial robust evaluation of subordinate leaders as well as maintain a continuous pro-social environment to detect, prevent, and rehabilitate or remove a hubris-afflicted subordinate in order to preserve the primacy of the objective. This paper

1

advocates the existence of hubris as an inherent character trait, through definition and history, with recurrent linkages to significant lost national treasure and blood. While numerous examples exist in which hubris adversely affected military operations, the challenge for combatant commanders will be to ensure highly motivated subordinates are properly balanced in their effort to achieve mission objectives in support of the overall strategic and operational objectives. A subordinate driven by hubris, a dangerous illusion of personal greatness, will endanger mission objectives and the combatant commander's ability to achieve the greater operational and strategic objectives.

Three historical cases provide demonstrations in which hubris led to disastrous strategic effects: Alcibiades' expedition to Sicily during the Peloponnesian War, Napoleon Bonaparte's attempt to conquer Russia in 1812, and L. Paul Bremer's Iraqi government transitional leadership. Alcibiades provides an example of hubris, cultivated prior to access of powerful leadership positions, leading to a life in search of affirming his glory and perceived greatness in the world through the collection of greater power.[6] In contrast, Napoleon's adolescence does not contain the same early lessons of grandeur, as experienced by Alcibiades, yet gradually develops a heightened level of hubris in turning stunning victories across the battlefield into a collapse of the French army and, ultimately, the French government. Finally, Bremer enters the leadership role in Iraq with hubris in full bloom, and his access to power acts as the conduit for an increase in the magnitude of negative consequences. All three examples provide a foundation for the claim that hubris exists as an inherent character flaw and an individual's access to power serves only to set the azimuth of impact. While eradicating hubris entirely from an operational leader's character is implausible, leaders at all levels can strengthen their awareness of this trait and prevent squandered opportunities.

The first line of defense against the perils of hubris is an understanding of its very existence as part of the larger context of the human character. From the Christian religious origins of human beings as told by the Bible, Eve falls prey to the temptation offered by the seducer to partake in the forbidden fruit so that "ye shall be as gods".[7] This story of man and woman introduces the possibility that the combination of greed and narcissism exists universally in all human beings, and we currently define this as hubris. Resulting from the initial flaw of man, Genesis 3:17 establishes a punishment for man ("cursed is the ground for thy sake; in sorrow shalt thou eat of it all the days of thy life") to counterbalance the transgression, thereby introducing a great struggle inherent in all human beings.[8] The Bible's troubled origins of man suggests the existence of inherent character traits within each individual, yet common to all, and the potentially costly penalties for hubris-influenced behavior.

Early Greek civilization recognized the existence of hubris, albeit with a view towards a grave criminal act centered on self-gratification at the expense of others.[9] This character trait existed regardless of the amount of power possessed, highlighting the existence of a character flaw in everyone, causing individuals to compromise even their most core interests.[10] Greek tragedy frequently explored hubris, through sensationalized stories of powerful figures, in a way that demonstrated all men and women were equally vulnerable.[11] Examples of the tragic flaw of hubris as the root cause of man's demise include Homer's The Iliad, Sophocles' Oedipus & Antigone, Icarus mythology, and the many works depicting the Trojan War. These stories surrounding the illusion of self-aggrandizement reflect a perilous risk that grows with greater danger as one attains more power. Hubris is displayed by an individual through his or her effort to seek revenge, capture personal honor, or prove greatest over others. Greek literature reveals awareness that hubris is an all-present danger. While the individuals in the stories were capable of great accomplishments, hubris remained an eternal threat with spectacular destructive consequences.

These mythological writings and stories point to a recurring warning regarding the existence and dangers of hubris, so that we may be aware and avoid fatal consequences.[12] Recent exploration of human behavior has asserted that human behavior may be influenced by innate pre-determined factors. For example, Carl Jung explored human behavior and suggested behaviors are embedded into the human construct and inherited as part of our preexistent programming. This embedded human construct, or collective unconscious, does not develop individually and is an enduring part of human nature.[13] Extrapolating from Jung's exploration, hubris could be an enduring component of human behavior, suggesting this potential character flaw is an inherent part of each individual.

As further corroboration for hubris as part of our inherent character, studies have recognized that most people overestimate their capabilities and underestimate the abilities of others.[14] This self-exaggeration appears to confirm the inherent characteristics of hubris within man manifested by a sense of positive illusion of one's self regarding his or her invulnerability to risk and control over events. This suggests hubris potentially exists as a part of the collective unconscious.

Owen and Davidson explored instances of hubris among UK prime ministers and US presidents' during the post-WWII era.[15] The power entrusted to these various leaders enabled the negative effects of their hubris to have widespread impacts. However, their access to power served as a stimulus for a flourishing of hubris revealing the character flaw that already existed. Petit and Bollaert argue that hubris affects leaders beyond the political arena, and that the negative aspects of hubris are present wherever leaders and power are in action, such as chief executive officer's (CEO) in the global business environment or commanders in the U.S. military environment.[16] In the majority of environments, these leaders are appointed, authorized, and instructed to lead others in such a way as to create a sense of difference from those that follow them. This hierarchy creates a relationship allowing leaders to act in a manner separate from their subordinates, leading from an exalted position to 'command' their subordinates, and for the subordinates to accept this leader-follower relationship. If unchallenged, the leader is exposed to an environmental stimulus for the character traits of hubris to grow in scope and impact. The Icarus mythology highlights the challenge for leaders operating in environments fertile for the growth of hubris: do not fly too high and do not fly too low.

Recognizing that hubris is a character flaw in all human beings, the outcomes achieved by leaders do not suggest that the only outcome is of negative consequences. An examination of leaders responsible for or party to exceptional failures serves as a method to continue reinforcing the moral commonly found in the early Greek mythology. While spectacular collapses capture the imagination, hopefully they are caricatures overshadowing the majority of individuals capable of adequately avoiding hubris-influenced behavior.

With a presumed case for the existence of hubris as an inherent universal human character trait, a framework exists in the military for hubris-influenced behavior to negatively impact operations. Starting from strategic guidance as one representation of potential military cultural perceptions, President Obama published the "Sustaining U.S. Global Leadership: Priorities for 21st Century Defense," dated 3 January 2012.[17] The document seeks "American global leadership" and "military superiority" with an eye toward keeping the U.S. "the greatest force for freedom and security that the world has ever known."[18] The mission espoused by this guidance provides the context for individuals to see the world with a disproportionate concern for image, inflated self-perception, and a mission of a higher calling beyond judgment of man. If an individual internalizes an exaggerated view of self based on military culture perceptions, then the conduit for access to extensive power rests within the Department of Defense doctrine.

Distinct lines of command are outlined as fundamental principles for joint command and control, with clear guidance that a commander has the authority and responsibility "for the attainment of these missions."[19] Combatant commanders possess a heightened level of authority based on the Unified Campaign Plan and Title 10, United States Code.[20] Doctrine recognizes the challenges of war through fog and friction, with the burden and art of war resting upon the shoulders of the commander. Joint Publication 3-0 reinforced this view by stating:

> A commander's perspective of the challenge at hand is broader and more comprehensive than the staff's due to interaction with civilian leaders; senior, peer, subordinate, and supporting commanders; and interorganizational partners. Clear commander's guidance and intent *enriched by the commander's experience and intuition* [emphasis added] are common to high-performing units.[21]

Doctrine also includes key references to the importance of the commander as the "central figure"[22] and "certain key planning elements require the commander's participation and decisions."[23] These are critical aspects integral to the effectiveness of combatant commanders given the hierarchal nature of the U.S. military. While doctrine has provided the framework, the 3 April 2012 Mission Command White Paper authored by General Martin Dempsey, Chairman of the Joint Chiefs of Staff, strengthens the primacy of the commander throughout the Department of Defense and challenging "every leader" to "act aggressively and independently."[24] These passages have not been identified for purposes of adjustment in order to remove the primacy of the commander, but rather as key indicators of the potential for culture attributes within the military contributing to the cultivation of an individual's hubristic character flaw.

The power entrusted to commanders, and combatant commanders explicitly, should warrant continuous performance assessment given the depth and scope of impact should the individual become consumed by the glamour of his or her position. With the proposed inherent nature of hubris and the relative importance given current U.S. military doctrine, historical cases reveal the danger associated with hubris in individuals occupying powerful leadership positions.

Hubris finds a unique breeding ground in the life story of Alcibiades as a lesson in the addiction of hubris when cultivated at an early age without regard to its destructive nature, particularly when behavior is relatively unopposed. The tragic flaw of hubris within Alcibiades leads to an operational failure of Athenian forces in Sicily and, arguably, directly to the strategic failure of his native Athenian government. Dangers are inherent in a political environment in which an individual afflicted by hubris is afforded exceptional access to power.[25]

Alcibiades is the son of a wealthy warrior, Clienias. The combination of the Clienias' high honor of death on the battlefield and wealth results in Alcibiades being raised by a powerful family, which includes Pericles and Ariphron. Additionally, Socrates (a prominent philosopher in Athens), who recognizes the dazzling beauty and charm exhibited by Alcibiades, befriends Alcibiades and maintains a strong bond throughout their lives. Alcibiades upbringing forms him into a young man with a strong passion to "challenge others and gain the upper hand over his rivals."[26] As a matter of principle, Alcibiades views himself with supreme confidence and envisions his desire for grandeur to be mirrored as that of the Greek city-state. Alcibiades possesses the wealth, birth status, and warrior honor (not to mention his charm and beauty) driving a personal mission for admiration and actions based in winning glory in order to enhance his personal image. Notwithstanding the favorable contemplation of his capability to win in battle, Alcibiades has visions of taking Carthage, Libya, Italy, and the Peloponnesian, well before Athens has successfully secured Sicily.[27]

Alcibiades' embrace of hubris is near absolute, as witnessed by his jealousy of Nicias. Alcibiades seeks to improve his personal image through a concerted effort to disgrace Nicias.[28] With respect to operational consequences, the conflict between Alcibiades and Nicias dooms the expedition to Sicily to catastrophic failure, with tremendous losses to the Athenian military, as well as the death of Nicias. Of strategic consequence, Athens is critically vulnerable to Sparta. Lysander exploits this weakness and, subsequently, Athens is unable to resist conquest.[29]

This historical case reflects the strategic impact when hubris is unbridled at the operational level. Alcibiades failed to acknowledge the significant, strategic danger of Sparta at the figurative doorstep of Athens and focused his personal desire (distracting the Athenian community) toward commingled personal and national greatness and glory in far away lands. The tremendous power conveyed upon Alcibiades served to reinforce his character flaw of hubris.

Additionally, this scenario is also a lesson in the jeopardy associated with placing an individual, raised with a disproportionate concern for personal image and contempt for others, into positions of unchecked power. The intoxication of hubris remained with Alcibiades even after he fled Athens during the Sicilian expedition to seek refuge in Sparta. Despite the dramatic reduction in his access to power within Athens, hubris drove Alcibiades to new power venues in Sparta through self-gratification, exaggerated personal image, and a conflated zeal for greatness as his righteous place in the world. The upbringing of Alcibiades highlights the dangers when barriers to hubris are not reinforced at an early age. However, barriers fortified early in life may not be sufficient in preventing hubris from dominating behavior.

Napoleon Bonaparte's historical context introduces the ever-present negative influence of

hubris, despite an upbringing capable of instilling boundaries, and the danger of rapid victories

without consideration for opposing viewpoints. His upbringing in a modest noble family of

Corsican origin (a region with Italian lineage recently added to the French empire), coupled with

early religious schooling, should have reinforced the boundaries necessary to contain hubris-

influenced behavior.[30] However, as history would reveal, Napoleon develops an incessant desire

for power, glory, and control across the European continent.

Through a series of early military victories, Napoleon builds an inflated ego

(disproportioned view of personal image).[31] Napoleon slowly develops a cult of personality and

the walls of internal balance are demolished. Napoleon readily accepted uncritical praise leading

him to develop an inflated image of self with nation and to visualize a world devoted to his self-

gratification, reflecting the merging of self and nation as one.[32] When requested to join the

revolution, Napoleon joined the effort and seized near complete power over France, effectively

outmaneuvering the very individuals who asked him for support. With this new national-level

position of authority, Napoleon championed national pride and glory among the French people as

well as projected a vision of himself as an ancient hero or knight throughout the growing empire

of France. Napoleon's insatiable personal drive to enhance his image, as well as his contempt

for others, could have served as a driving force behind the march to Moscow, as the only

European monarch not subjugated by Napoleon was the Russian Czar.[33]

The perceived personal greatness of Napoleon, and of France, turned eastward to expand

the French empire into Russia. Napoleon achieved the operational objective to capture Moscow

on the backs of the Grand Army with great loss of blood and treasure resulting from the constant

brutal fighting, expansive geographic distance, and harsh environmental conditions within

Russia.[34] Napoleon need only claim the victory by establish a governing body and conducting an operational pause. This pause arguably would have enabled his forces to recover from the arduous journey and replenish their strained logistics. Instead, primarily due to the Russians failure to conduct a 'proper' acknowledgement of surrender, Napoleon perceived a great personal slight and ordered the remaining French troops (many were not native French) to pillage and sack Moscow.[35] Napoleon failed to secure military gains within Russia primarily due to his decisions as a result of hubris-influenced behavior.

The combination of detrimental decisions and an overextended military position resulted in a vulnerable French army becoming a tragic victim of Napoleon's hubris. Looting served to unite the Russian people against the French army and significantly degraded popular support from the French people. The possibility for a quick victory in Moscow existed, yet turned into a protracted war overlooking the warnings of Sun Tzu: "There is no instance of a country having benefited from prolonged war."[36] Unable to sustain combat operations, and recognizing that the French army no longer possessed the capacity to hold its geographic gains, Napoleon led his troops back to France under the banner of failure.

Despite having confidants and advisors among his inner circle, Napoleon developed a sense of higher calling while engulfed by arrogance and self-entitlement. Clearly, pride is an indispensable driving force encouraging Napoleon to strive for achievement.[37] However, Napoleon raced past pride early in his military career and crossed into the clutches of hubris prior to assuming national leadership. This new position served to ratchet up the magnitude of penalty for hubris behavior. The principle of supremacy of the military objective, and the appropriate recognition of the Clausewitz's culminating point of victory,[38] was overshadowed by Napoleon's personal objective (recognition of his superiority). The grand master of strategy and tactical brilliance allowed hubris to cloud his mind, capturing defeat despite an overwhelming opportunity for victory.

Hubris exhibited by Napoleon reflects the eternal struggle within each individual. For combatant commanders, Napoleon highlights the need for continuous reevaluation to preserve the supremacy of the military objective. However, Napoleon occupied a national leadership position, and would potentially only be restrained by personal, internal effort or by total popular revolt. At lower levels of authority, superior leaders possess an opportunity to conduct the continuous evaluation of themselves and their subordinates in order to protect against the rise of future Napoleon-like individuals.

L. Paul Bremer offers a glimpse into a contemporary example of a rare blend of hubris reflecting the projection of ambition and confidence without empathy or humility.[1] Bremer affords a lesson for future leaders of the need to hold their subordinates accountable for hubris-influenced behavior. If the failure is egregious, commanders must be willing to hold subordinates accountable and remove them from the position of power. While Bremer was operating with the presumed oversight of President Bush and Defense Secretary Rumsfeld, the environment Bremer operated within possessed no strategic checks or balances to offset his dangerous, impulsive decision making process.[39] As identified by Parrington, Bremer may have

---

[1] Defense Secretary Rumsfeld appointed Bremer (a State Department diplomat) in 2003 after numerous other Department of State recommendations were rejected by Rumsfeld (Younes & McMahon, 2003). Bremer could have served as an independent leader of the Coalition Provisional Authority (CPA). Instead, Bremer appeared to endorse the same viewpoints as his conservative superiors (Younes & McMahon, 2003). In fact, Bremer appeared to marginalize contrary viewpoints presented by Department of State, U.S. Army, and independent advisors (Jones, 2006). Potentially because of this commonality, Bremer operated without direct oversight from President Bush and Secretary Rumsfeld, who appeared to have conflicting visions yet failed to address the differences (Hirsh, 2006). Bremer's initial decisions, independently made and passively accepted (arguably) by superiors, created an unemployed mass consisting of over half a million men, armed and with knowledge of munition cache locations (Carruthers, 2007). None of the senior leaders at the time (Cheney, Rumsfeld, Wolfowitz, Rice, or Bremer) consented to questioning regarding the fateful decisions made by Bremer (Carruthers, 2007). Bremer has recently deflected blame for his decisions toward President Bush and Secretary Rumsfeld based on their lack of action when Bremer requested additional support (Martin, 2013). However, when Bremer knew of the disconnects during his tenure at CPA chief, he failed to resolve the differences leading to the tragic impact of his hubris-influenced behavior (Hirsh, 2006).

been selected purposely and encouraged in his behavior as reflected by the arrogance of his superiors.[40] Bremer departed Iraq in 2004 without being held accountable for hubris-influenced decisions which clearly caused significant damage to the U.S. in all aspects of the instrument of national power.[41]

Prior to assumption as the leader of the Iraqi Coalition Provisional Authority (CPA), Bremer was a career American diplomat with a distinguished record of success, and a recognized expert in the fields of terrorism and homeland security.[42] Additionally, his image potentially reflected a "patrician tradition going back to Dean Acheson, Henry Stemson, and John McCloy."[43] With a history of success and a cultivated expertise in diplomacy, Bremer inspired loyalty and affection from those who worked for him.

Bremer took charge of the CPA in 2003 and his impact upon Iraq, as well as the international community, was immediately felt. While he was one of the few diplomatic employees to embark outside the heavily fortified Baghdad Green Zone, Bremer failed to build a consensus with Iraqis nor did he allow anyone to challenge his views or assumptions.[44] His first months of leadership embarked on following the post-World War II German reconstruction model. Bremer's focus was on establishing a new constitution, creating an interim transition government, and handing over sovereignty as quickly as possible.[45] Despite the lessons learned from the German reconstruction and disregarding the advice of his team, Bremer issued two orders that would have substantial negative strategic impacts.[46]

First, similar to the failed de-Nazification direction in Germany, Bremer ordered the de-Baathification of Iraqi government employees. This order effectively removed a significant majority of personnel in key local and regional positions. Basic services (e.g., water, electricity, trash, police) for the Iraqi people began to fail and the infrastructure necessary to conduct daily life collapsed. This order drove the local populace to become disenfranchised with any Iraqi government and view the American presence as a form of occupation.[47] Second, Bremer ordered the disbanding of the Iraqi Army immediately. Disgruntled soldiers walked away from their posts without turning in their weapons and went home to the chaos caused by Bremer's first decision. Iraq was flooded with unemployed, armed young men, with disproportionate free time, and a negative perspective toward the Americans.[48] The price of inflicted upon the U.S. military and the local Iraqi population would be tremendous.

Hubris is manifested within Bremer through his decisions, a reluctance to consider contrary opinions, and a self-principle above critique from others. One sees the simple form of arrogance in his denial to consider the opinions of Iraqi government leaders consideration for courses of action.[49] Additionally, Bremer's CPA leadership style reflects an inflated self-image comingled with that of the Iraqi nation as reflected in his singular, uncontestable vision of future Iraqi governance structure.[50] Narcissism also exists in his actions taken to enhance his personal image, particularly with his decision to remain true to the failed policies of the German reconstruction.[51] Bremer failed to properly recognize the operational environment, clouded by his perceptions, when he assumed lead of the CPA.[52]

During Bremer's tenure, his unchecked decision-making process led to Bremer failing to recognize actual control slipping away from the CPA, as well as a denial of his role in the instability of Iraq. Hubris retains a measure of influence long after Iraq as evident when Bremer refers to his departure from Iraq as Liberation Day, his release from the responsibilities of the CPA, and that the remaining floundering Iraqi government is now solely responsible for making the new republic work (despite being seriously handicapped by a growing insurgency).[53] In 2006, Bremer wrote of his experience and largely failed to acknowledge the criticisms of his work, and attempted to shift blame (as if he is beyond disparagement) to Defense Secretary Rumsfeld.[54] Hubris might also suggest that Bremer's actions were taken because he viewed himself among the great diplomatic leaders, such as John McCloy.[55]

Given a sufficient case has been made confirming the natural and eternal existence of hubris within every individual, the three historical cases reflects the dangers every combatant commander should find vitally important. First, Alcibiades teaches combatant commanders the utility in identifying subordinates seized by hubris prior to placing them in positions of greater power and responsibility. Commanders must attempt to instill humility and rationale self-image through direct mentorship and establishing long-term relationships between the subordinate and outside actors to provide candid guidance and feedback to the subordinate, as well as to the commander. Kerfoot advises leaders to foster a trusted sidekick relationship in order to keep an individual properly grounded, particularly in keeping a realistic perception of the environment around the leader.[56] President Abraham Lincoln serves as an example of a leader utilizing the trusted relationship to balance the negative aspects of hubris. He frequently sought honest and forthright counsel from his cabinet and advisors, many of whom were rivals during his presidential nomination campaign.[57] In military practice, commanders could establish periodic documented feedback with their subordinates and include additional feedback from an assigned trusted peer to the subordinate. This multi-level feedback could foster a more complete, honest counsel to the subordinate and enable the commander a greater understanding of the subordinate. Combatant commanders must then be willing to deny subordinates leadership positions when the multi-level feedback does not deliver confidence that acceptable boundaries are part of a subordinate's capacity. This difficult decision is necessary before the ill effects of hubris-influenced leadership are felt damaging strategic or operational objectives.

Second, Napoleon reinforces the critical requirement for combatant commanders to maintain a robust continuous evaluation process of subordinates. Button recognizes that even the wisest can learn new things without a loss in personal image.[58] The ever-present character flaw of hubris, existing as part of human nature, can be restrained by a determined effort to remain open to new ideas and concepts from others. The openness balances power exposure, potentially minimizing the catalyst for hubris to grow. Identification of hubris must take into account the perception of the commander as well as a complete, 360-degree depiction including the opinions of peers and subordinates. Reflecting an opportunity for hubris to be properly identified, General Martin Dempsey, the current U.S. Chairman of the Joint Chiefs of Staff, has advocated for a 360-degree review of military leaders.[59] A well-rounded evaluation of the subordinate is a critical aspect verifying the authenticity of a leader, potentially identifying hubris-influenced behavior, and establishing any potential re-education plan.[60] Where 'hubris-creep' is revealed, commanders should take action to reinforce humility as a core guiding principle, particularly during the decision-making process, and promote a rationale self-image in order to avoid similarities to the Alcibiades case study. The criticality of leadership demands commanders be willing to remove those unable or unwilling to maintain barriers to 'hubris-creep'. Commanders are sufficient justification to remove a subordinate from a leadership role based on the negative affects of hubris-influenced behavior. However, commanders should also be sufficiently justified to remove a subordinate from a leadership role based on a "lack of confidence" when feedback reveals a trace of hubris-influenced behavior and the subordinate fails to improve behavior after intervention. Fortunately, in our current political and economic environment, suitable replacements with a healthy balance of pride and humility can be found.

Third, Bremer illustrates the penalty when leaders, political and military, fail to keep hubris-influenced individuals from positions of power or fail to maintain sufficient oversight of hubris-influence individuals to avoid catastrophic strategic and operational blunders. Combatant commanders should not develop a delusional sense of security that hubris will not corrupt their subordinates. Hubris connotes a level of anti-social behavior in appreciation for self-image and contempt for others.[61] For leaders to allow subordinates to progress unchecked over a period of significant time, without constructive critique, and assume subordinates will avoid hubris also reflects arrogance and denial of the existing strategic danger of hubris.

Continuous communication and inclusion within the social environment serves to anchor the individual in a healthy consideration for the value of others and regulate personal image perceptions.[62] During World War II, enabled by a robust social environment among senior leaders, General Eisenhower and General Marshall were able to identify a superior candidate, General Lucius Clay, to lead the reconstruction of western Germany.[63] The moral courage exhibited by General Clay enabled the avoidance of hubristic behaviors, keeping the supremacy of the military and civilian objectives, ultimately leading to a sustainable, successful Germany.[64] For example, General Clay regularly consulted with the appointed German ministers as well as conducted frequent press meetings to ensure a free-flow exchange of ideas and messages.[65]

The same measures suggested as required duties for a combatant commander also present opportunities for individuals to adopt as a form of self-responsibility. Failure to listen to others or to contribute serious consideration for outside views is one significant detrimental behavior attributable to hubris.[66] This behavior could be a result of an exaggerated sense of greatness within ones self coupled with sentiment of contempt for others. Petit and Bollaert propose individuals strive to include reverence as "a state of profound ... awareness of and respect for

16

that which surpasses us, and … a moral connection with the other members of the human community." [67] Every leader must seek to be part of the social community, effectively obtaining and considering varying (with an eye towards opposing) views, and weighing personal ambition within the context of the impact upon the organization and people around them.

Leaders with access to military instruments of power occupy a position of tremendous responsibility and potentially perilous power. Military leaders will find themselves in these very positions, in a culture of 'mission command', entrusted by their superiors to accomplish the assigned mission objectives without direct guidance. The inherent power of the position coupled with an environment conditional upon the 'brilliance' of the commander creates a breeding ground for hubris to capture the fragile leader. Each military leader has a personal responsibility to frame his or her behavior in defense against hubris. With each individual possessing varying levels of defense against hubris, combatant commanders must embrace a pro-social atmosphere complete with a robust continuous reevaluation process. Current combatant commanders may perceive these recommendations to be basic measures commonly applied at their level. However, the military's growing culture of decentralized execution warrants renewed verification that subordinates will continue to embrace proper measures against hubris as they rise in responsibility and power access. This paper is not monumental but deserving of attention, particularly given the repetitive nature hubris-influenced behavior appears in senior military leaders with catastrophic implications at the strategic level.

NOTES

1. Julius Caesar, Thinkexist.com website, Accessed 15 March 2013.
    http://thinkexist.com/quotation/it-s-only-hubris-if-i-fail/631340.html

2. S. Hashmi and S. Lee, *Ethics and Weapons of Mass Destruction: Religious and Secular Perspectives* (New York, NY: Oxford University Press, 2004).

3. David Owen and Jonathan Davidson, "Hubris Syndrome: An acquired personality disorder? A study of US Presidents and UK Prime Ministers over the last 100 years," *Oxford Journals*, 6 May 2009.
    http://brain.oxfordjournals.org/content/early/2009/02/12/brain.awp008.full

4. Oxford English Dictionary Online, s.v. "Arrogance," Accessed 13 May 2013,
    http://dictionary.oed.com/cgi/entry

5. Louise Carr, "Hubris Syndrome – Psychologists Discover New Personality Disorder Among Political Leaders," *zoomHealth*, 30 October 2010.
    http://www.zoomhealth.net/HubrisSyndrome.html

6. Robert B. Strassler, ed. *The Landmark Thucydides* (New York: The Free Press, 1996), 6:43

7. Online Bible, King James version, Genesis 3:5, Accessed 31 March 2013.
    http://www.biblica.com/bibles/chapter/?verse-Genesis+3&version=kjv

8. Ibid.

9. Aristotle, "Rhetoric," *Perseus-Tufts*. 2.2.1378B, Accessed 31 March 2013.
    http://www.perseus.tufts.edu/cgi-bin/ptest?doc=Perseus%3Atest%3A1999.01.0060;query=chapter%3D%2317;layout=;loc=2.1.1

10. Barbara W. Tuchman, *The March of Folly: from Troy to Vietnam* (New York: Ballantine Books, 1985): 46.

11. John Jones, *On Aristotle and Greed Tragedy* (New York: Oxford University Press, 1962): 88.

12. Diane Trumbull, "Hubris: A primal danger," *Psychiatry* 73, 4 (2010): 342.

13. Ibid., 344.

14. Dominic D.P. Johnson and James H. Fowler, "The evolution of overconfidence," *Nature* 477 (2011): 317-320.

15. David Owen and Jonathan Davidson, "Hubris Syndrome: An acquired personality disorder? A study of US Presidents and UK Prime Ministers over the last 100 years," *Oxford Journals*, 6 May 2009. http://brain.oxfordjournals.org/content/early/2009/02/12/brain.awp008.full

16. Valerie Petit and Helen Bollaert, "Flying too close to the sun? Hubris among CEOs and how to prevent it," *Journal of Business Ethics* 108 (2012): 265-283.

17. Department of Defense. *Sustaining U.S. Global Leadership: Priorities for 21st Century Defense.* January 2012. http://www.defense.gov/releases/release.aspx?releaseid=14992.

18. Ibid.

19. Chairman, U.S. Joint Chiefs of Staff, *Joint Operations,* Joint Publication 1, Washington DC: CJCS, 20 March 2009, xv.

20. Ibid., III-15.

21. Chairman, U.S. Joint Chiefs of Staff, *Joint Operations,* Joint Publication 3-0, Washington DC: CJCS, 11 August 2011, xii.

22. Ibid., xiii.

23. Ibid.

24. Ibid., *Mission Command White Paper*, Washington DC: CJCS, 3 April 2012

25. Eric Hoyer, *Alcibiades' Challenge to Democratic Politics* (ProQuest dissertations and theses, 2011): 16.

26. Plutarch. *The Rise and Fall of Athens: Nine Greek Lives.* Translated with an introduction by Ian Scott-Kilvert (New York and London: Penguin, 1960): 246.

27. Ibid., 260.

28. Ibid., 246.

29. Ibid., 296.

30. Max Lyons, *Napoleon Bonaparte and the Legacy of the French Revolution* (New York: St. Martin's Press, 1994).

31. Mark J. Kroll, Leslie A. Toombs, and Peter Wright, "Napoleon's tragic march home from Moscow: Lessons in hubris," *The Academy of Management Executive* 14, 1 (2000), 121.

32. Charles Esdaile, "Spain 1808-Iraq 2003: Some Thoughts on the Use and Abuse of History," *The Journal of Military History* 74, 1 (2010), 183.

33. Kroll, Toombs, and Wright, "Napoleon's tragic march home from Moscow: Lessons in hubris," 121.

34. Ibid., 122.

35. Max Lyons, "Napoleon Bonaparte and the Legacy of the French Revolution," 188.

36. Sun Tzu. *The Art of War.* Samuel B. Griffith, trans. (Oxford: Oxford University Press, 1980).

37. Kroll, Toombs, and Wright, "Napoleon's traffic march home from Moscow: Lessons in hubris," 117.

38. Carl von Clausewitz, *On War,* Michael Howard and Peter Paret, eds. and trans. (Princeton Univesity Press, 1976).

39. Robert Younes, and Janet McMahon,"Post-Saddam U.S. leaders Garner, Bremer, and Chalabi all have Neocon ties," *The Washington Post on Middle East Affairs* 22 (2003): 12,59.

40. James R. Parrington, *Operational Failures Caused by Arrogant Leaders.* Research paper, U.S. Naval War College, Joint Military Operations Department, Newport, 2008.

41. Hugh Gusterson, "An Education in Occupation," *Radical Teacher* 94 (2012): 58-60,79

42. Michael Hirsh, "Paul Bremer was just following instructions," *The Washington Monthly* 38, 3 (2006): 32-33.

43. Ibid., 31.

44. Eric Stover, Hanny Megally, and Hania Mufti, "Bremer's "Gordian Knot": Transitional Justice and the U.S. Occupation of Iraq," *Human Rights Quarterly* 27, 3. (2005): 834-835.

45. Hirsh, "Paul Bremer was just following instructions," 32-33.

46. Stover, Megally, and Mufti, "Gordian Knot": Transitional Justice and the U.S. Occupation of Iraq," 844.

47. Ibid., 846-847.

48. Paul Martin, *We made major strategic mistakes. But I still think Iraqis are far better of.* The Independent [London(UK)], 19 March 2013: 26.

49. Stover, Megally, and Mufti, "Bremer's "Gordian Knot": Transitional Justice and the U.S. Occupation of Iraq," 834.

50. Ibid.

51. Hirsh, "Paul Bremer was just following instructions," 33.

52. Ibid.

53. Ibid.

54. Ibid., 32.

55. Ibid., 33.

56. Karlene M. Kerfoot, "Leaders, Self-Confidence, and Hubris: What's the Difference?" *On Leadership, Nursing Economics* 28, 5 (2010), 349.

57. Donovan Campbell, "The Learning and Leadership Accelerator – Humility," *Credera*, 25 June 2012. http://blog.credera.com/topic/management-consulting/the-learning-and-leadership-accelerator-humility/, and Rabbi Joel Fleekop, "Lincoln and Moses: Humility and Leadership," *Congregation Shir Hadash*, accessed 1 May 2013. http://www.shirhadash.org/rabbi/11/02/19/lincoln.html

58. Mark E. Button, "Hubris Breeds the Tyrant": The Anti-Politics of Hubris from Thebes to Abu Ghraib*," Law, Culture and the Humanities* 8, 2 (2011), 331.

59. Thom Shanker, "Conduct at Issue as Military Officers Face a New Review," *The New York Times*, 31 April 2013. http://www.nytimes.com/2013/04/14/us/militarys-top-officers-face-review-of-their-character.html?pagewanted=all&_r=0

60. Valerie Petit and Helen Bollaert, "Flying too close to the sun? Hubris among CEOs and how to prevent it," *Journal of Business Ethics* 108 (2012), 273.

61. Dianne Trumbull, "Hubris: A Primal Danger," *Psychiatry* 73, 4 (2010), 347.

62. Kerfoot, "Leaders, Self-Confidence, and Hubris: What's the Difference?" 351.

63. Andrews J. Sullivan, *General Lucius D. Clay: Operational Leadership in a Post-Combat Environment.* Research paper, U.S. Naval War College, Joint Military Operations Department, Newport, 2009: 1.

64. Ibid., 15.

65. Peter Grose, "The boss of occupied Germany: General Lucius D. Clay," *Foreign Affairs* 77, 4 (1998) 179-185. OmniFile Full Text Select (H.W. Wilson), EBSCOhost (accessed May 15, 2013).

66. M.C. Anderson and A.M. Marak, "Pancho Villa's revolution by headlines," *Canadian Journal of History* 34, 3 (2000), 605-608.

67. Petit and Bollaert, "Flying too close to the sun? Hubris among CEOs and how to prevent it," *Journal of Business Ethics* 108 (2012), 275.

SELECTED BIBLIOGRAPHY

Abshire, David M. "Presidential Hubris," *National Forum* 80, no. 1 (2000): 45-48.

Anonymous. "Ba'athists Back in Iraq," *The New American* 20, 10. (2004): 9.

Barnett, Neil. "Disbanding the Army," *Middle East* 350 (2004): 11.

Bergland, Christopher. "The Athlete's Way," *Psychology Today* 3 March 2013. http://www.psychologytoday.com/blog/the-athletes-way/201303/the-sweet-spot-between-hubris-and-humility.htm

Bray, Robert. "Abraham Lincoln and the Two Peters," *Journal of the Abraham Lincoln Association* 22, 2 (2001): 27-49.

Carruthers, Susan L. "Question Time: The Iraq War Revisited," *Cineaste* 32, 4 (2007): 12-17.

Cooper, Wesley W. *What does the military need to do to ensure that our operational leaders are prepared to meet the challenges of the 21st century?* Research paper, U.S. Naval War College, Joint Military Operations Department, Newport, 2009.

Doherty, Brian. "The Cult of the Presidency: America's Dangerous Devotion to Executive Power," *Freeman* 59, 2 (2009): 42-43.

Doty, Joseph, "Humility as a Leadership Attribute," *Military Review*, Sept-Oct (2000). Accessed 1 May 2013. http://au.af.mil/au/awc/awcgate/milreview/doty.pdf

Grose, Peter. "The Boss of Occupied Germany: General Lucius D. Clay," *Foreign Affairs* 77, 4 (1998): 179-185.

Guelzo, Allen C. "The Prudence of Abraham Lincoln," *First Things* 159 (2006): 11-13.

Hitchens, Christopher. "Blood for No Oil!" *The Atlantic Monthly;* May, 297, 4 (2006): 133-136.

Horne, A. *How far from Austerlitz? Napoleon 1805-1815.* New York: MacMillan, 1996.

Jones, Frank L. "Rolling the Dice of War," *International Journal* 61, 4 (2006): 945-958.

Karrasch, Angela I., & Halpin, Stanley M. "Feedback on 360 Degree Leader AZIMUTH Check Assessment Conducted at Fort Clayton, Panama," *U.S. Army Research Institute for the Behavioral and Social Sciences*, Fort Leavenworth, KS, March 1999. http://www.dtic.mil/cgi-bin/GetTRDoc?AD=ADA361832&Location=U2&doc=GetTRDoc.pdf

Lamberti, Marjorie. "General Lucius Clay, German Politicians, and the Great Crisis During the Making of West Germany's Constitution," *German Politics and Society* 27, 4 (2009): 24-50.

Lefever, Ernest W. "A Just Conflict, Ethically Pursued," *Global Dialogue* 3, 4 (2001): 71:79.

Meierhenrich, Jens. "The Ethics of Lustration," *Ethics & International Affairs* 20, 1. (2006): 99-120, 139.

Norton-Taylor, Richard, & Watt, Nicholas. *Iraq War was national disgrace, say former military chiefs: Rumsfeld, Bremer come in for particular criticism Alexander: war cause collapse in public trust.* The Guardian[London(UK)], 18 March 2013: 8.

Payne, Robert. *Hubris: A Study of Pride.* New York: Houghton-Mifflin, 2004.

Rid, Thomas. "The Winning Formula," *The Wilson Quarterly* 33, 4 (2009): 92-94

Rosby, Philippa. *The psychology of the powerful.* BBW News-Health, 6 Oct 2012. http://www.bbc.co.uk/news/health-19842100

Scherer, John L. *Locating Bin Laden.* USA Today, 139, 2788 (2011): 22-25.

Schimmel, Solomon. "Vices, virtues and sources of human strength in historical perspective," *Journal of Social and Clinical Psychology* 19, 1 (2000): 137-150.

Seabright, Paul. "The Imaginot Line," *Foreign Policy* Jan/Feb (2011): 84-87.

Shaw, George B. *George Bernard Shaw Quotes.* BrainyQuote, 31 March 2013. http://www.brainyquote.com/quotes/quotes/g/george_bernard_shaw.html

Tilghman, Andrew. "Dempsey: 350-dgree reviews could help select better leaders," *Army Times*, 1 May 2013. http://www.armytimes.com/article/20130501/NEWS/305010023/Dempsey-360-degree-reviews-could-help-select-better-leaders

Twair, Pat, & Twair, Samir. "Scholar ali Mazrui Calls on U.S. Democracy to Control American Military Empire," *The Washington Report on Middle East Affairs* 26, 5, (2007): 40-42.

Vego, Milan N. *Joint Operational Warfare: Theory and Practice.* Newport, RI: Naval War College Press, 20 September 2007

_____. *Operational Art.* Newport, RI: Naval War College Press, 2000.

Wood, Ellen M. "War without boundaries," *Canadian Dimension* 35, 6 (2001).

Xenophon. *Hellenica.* Trans. H.G. Dakyns. Newport, RI: Naval War College Press, 21 August 2008.

www.ingramcontent.com/pod-product-compliance
Lightning Source LLC
Chambersburg PA
CBHW081814280526
45789CB00008B/3129